# RANDOM THOUGHTS

*Reflections from the Mind of a Poet*

By Anthony Arnold

Cover design by Steamy Trails Publishing
Book design by Katrina Gurl

Anthony Arnold
Visit my website at author**anthonyarnold.webs**.com

Printed in the United States of America

First Printing: July 2014
Steamy Trails Publishing LLC

ISBN-13: 978-0692327494
ISBN-10: 0692327495

# RANDOM THOUGHTS

*Reflections from the Mind of a Poet*

# FOREWORD

The title of this book of poems, *RANDOM THOUGHTS: Reflections from the Mind of a Poet*, is the manifestation of feelings, thoughts and words onto paper with the heart stained in ink of Anthony's essence on every page. His complication this third time around are not only profound, but heart wrenching as well.

Over the last year, I've notices the growth in the range of Anthony's writing.  He has this amazing capability of captivating literary circles and poetry gathers alike. There are times when I read his work and think, *"Wow! Now, this is how poetry should really make you feel! Provoked, touched and enlightened."*  He is diverse, current and is always ready to shed light on any given situation rather it be historical events or very present ones.

Naturally, I was not at all surprised when Anthony was able to put together yet another book that touches my heart on an even grander scale than his first two book has. Which were: My People, Our Trials and Tribulations in 2012 and Urban Musings in 2013.

In my very personal opinion, I'd say that Author Anthony Arnold may very well one of the greatest poets of our time and I am more than happy to come to know his work, his poetry!

~ Katrina Gurl

# DEDICATION

I wish to dedicate this book to the women who made me who I am
My Great-grandmother, Maggie Nelson
My grandmother, Evelyn Livingston
My Wife, Penny Arnold
Without you I am nothing
Love you!

# CONTENTS

Foreword by Katrina Gurl .................................................4

Dedication.................................................................5

Acknowledgements .......................................................10

Introduction ............................................................11

Mom.....................................................................12

#BringBackOurGirls.......................................................13

Black Wall Street........................................................14

Blurred Lines ...........................................................18

The Barber Shop .........................................................19

24 hours ................................................................21

2013 ....................................................................22

A Storm is Coming........................................................24

A Summer of Discontent..................................................26

Amerikkka ...............................................................27

Homeless and Hungry.....................................................28

Homeless.................................................................29

Homeless Pt. 2 ..........................................................30

Homeless Pt. 3 ..........................................................31

Little Brothers .........................................................32

Destiny .................................................................33

Escape: A Story of Perseverance.........................................34

Escape: Pt. 2 – Desperation ........................................36

Escape: Pt. 3 - Resurrection ........................................38

Escape: Pt 4 - Redemption ........................................40

Mandela ........................................42

Our History ........................................44

Reflections ........................................45

Reflections Pt 2 ........................................46

Reflections 3: ........................................47

Rosewood ........................................49

Segregation ........................................50

A Conversation ........................................51

Do You Like the Rain? ........................................52

Love Jones ........................................54

Roses and Barbed Wire ........................................55

Self Love: An Erotic Short Story ........................................56

Tasty ........................................58

The 5 Tenets of Love ........................................59

The Jazz Singer ........................................61

Wedding Day ........................................62

Wedding Day Pt. 2 ........................................63

Wedding Day Pt. 3 ........................................64

What is Love? ........................................66

A Veteran's Sorrow ........................................67

A Veteran's Story .......................................................69

Bullied .......................................................................71

Don't Care any Mo' ..................................................73

Dred Scott ................................................................74

Hollow Dreams..........................................................75

Legacy .......................................................................76

On the Chain Gang ...................................................79

Pain ...........................................................................80

Pain Pt. 2 ..................................................................81

Rejoice ......................................................................82

Revenge .....................................................................83

Ships in the Night......................................................85

Strange fruit .............................................................86

Survival......................................................................87

The Book of Poetry ...................................................88

They Don't Care About Us ........................................89

Untitled #6 ................................................................90

Untitled 14 ................................................................91

Violated......................................................................92

Voices.........................................................................94

Voices Pt. 2................................................................95

Waterfalls...................................................................96

Watts..........................................................................97

Willie Lynch.............................................................99

My Muse ...............................................................101

On the Streets .......................................................103

Social confusion ....................................................104

A Storm is Coming Pt. 2 .......................................105

Running..................................................................107

Seeds of Destruction............................................108

Street Life..............................................................109

EXPRESSIONS .........................................................111

Anthony Arnold......................................................113

# ACKNOWLEDGEMENTS

First of all to God, for without him none of this is possible
To my poetic family. Thank you. You know who you are
To Jordan and Anthony, Love you guys!

To my publisher, Katrina, My sister, my friend

To my Great grand, and Grandmother

My strength, my inspiration
And to my heart, Penny Arnold. Thank you for your love and support.
Thanks for putting up with me. Love you babe!

And, to my poetic brethren, thank you for your love, your support
It's made me a better writer and a better person.

Thank you for going on this journey with me!
*Grasshopper humbly bows!*

# INTRODUCTION

This is my third book and in a lot of ways, the hardest to complete. My first two titles gave me clear direction, but when life takes sudden turns, so did my writing. For some reason, my ideas were all over the place this time. Nevertheless, the pieces selected within this book will cover all the terrain in my journey.

I thank all of you that have sojourned with me one more time.

Thank you,

~ Author Anthony Arnold

# MOM

This book is dedicated to the memory of my muse Marolyn Martin. On May 4, 1961, a 19 year old music major had a son. With the help of my grandmother, and great-grandmother, she taught him to get along in a world that was not his making. She taught him to apply his visions and the voices that he learned to hear in his head.

There was no one more proud when my first books, My People, Our Trials and Tribulations, and Urban Musings were released. She was looking forward to the release of this book. So this book is dedicated to her, My Muse, my mom. I miss you dearly.

Marolyn Martin
1942-2014

Your son,

Author Anthony Arnold

# #BRINGBACKOURGIRLS

In the cradle of civilization
A crisis is brewing
300 girls, taken from their school
Mothers not able to eat, families frantic

#bringbackourgirls

Boko haram, you say Allah directed you
You kill unarmed people, kidnap innocent girls
This does not sound like the Allah I know
May you all kafirwe salama*

#bringbackourgirls

You say you will sell them for $12
What man would buy a little girl?
For his pleasure, his enjoyment
For this they should burn in hell

#bringbackourgirls

Now there is outrage
Where once there was quiet
Now there is attention paid
Where was it before?

I would hope if any harm
Comes to these girls
That you are hunted to the ends of the earth
And Old Testament justice is applied slowly

Very slowly
#bringbackourgirls

*get ass fucked peacefully

13

# BLACK WALL STREET

*(A fictional account)*

May 31, 1921. That date will always remain etched into my mind and soul. You see that was the date that everything began to change. That everything was no longer the way it was. That we were no longer what we had been.
Our own.

*The beginning...*

My name is James Johnson, and I own a little store in Greenwood, a suburb of Tulsa in Oklahoma. A man named O.W. Gurley purchased land in 1906 with the express purpose of selling land to colored folk. This was unheard of at the time. A lot of prominent blacks lived in the area. I came west from New York looking to start a new life. To forget her. She who had broken my heart.
I purchased a store with the money that I brought with me and began to eke out an honest living. I even was able to love again. I married sweet Regina, a local girl and even though we were not able to have children, we adopted a child that had been left at the church steps. Our shop grew along with everything in the area. Prosperity was good. There were more airplanes owned by our people (6) than the whole state of Oklahoma (2). Everything was going well.

*Or so we thought. The elevator...*

May 30, 1921. A nice day in greenwood. Children playing, a band playing in the park. Business was good. What we didn't know that around the corner at the Drexel building action were playing out in a way that would change our way of life. Forever.
Dick Rowland, and Sarah Page. A worker and the elevator operator. According to whom you talked to were dating or not. No one actually knows what happed in that elevator, but we do know that the woman claimed rape, and he was arrested. It all went downhill from there. Arrested and put in jail, we were all in fear of his life. None of us thought that we would ever see him again.

*The riots...*

May 31, 1921. I opened my shop as I normally did. Spoke to some of the other shopkeepers, and waited for Regina to come down to the shop with little James like she always did. There was a buzz in the air about the arrested man sitting at the jail. There had been a mob of white folks down at the jail all night. So far nothing had happened.

*So far...*

I was in the shop talking with Regina when there was a big fuss outside. I walked out to see what was wrong. A group of blacks were arguing about the headlines in the paper. The Tulsa tribune put out the afternoon edition about 3. I wouldn't use that waste of a rag to wipe a bears butt. But others swore by it. The headline said "negro nabbed for attacking white girl in elevator. There was an ill wind blowing, and I needed to get my family away. I told Regina to take little James home and go to her family's house, that way they would be safe. I boarded up the store and waited.

*7:34 pm...*

I'm here at the jail with some other blacks trying to save this boy's life. The sheriff is determined there will be no lynching. The pawn shop owners opened their stores to the crowd. Now it's 700 angry whites to 30 blacks and the sheriff and his crew. They were determined that he would die and we were determined that he wasn't.

More blacks and more whites came to the court house. All were armed. Our being there was being taken as a "negro uprising". We were told to surrender our guns. Of course we said no. a shot was fired, no one knows by who.
It has begun.

*June 1, 1921, 01:00 am...*

We are in a fight for sure. Whites shooting innocent folks, burning shops. The National Guard is here, but have been no help. Over on Archer Street, there are buildings burning. Mobs would not let the fire department put the fires out, so the black owned businesses burn.

*Including mine...*

Blacks began to leave in a mass exodus to try and save themselves and their families. The mob fired on them as they wished. People were killed just trying to live. We tried to give as well as we got, but there were just too many. We could only do what we could
Try to survive.

*Daybreak...*

It arrived to the sound of a lonely whistle. And all hell broke loose. Fires had been burning since last night. None were allowed to be put out. Now with the sunrise a new threat arose.
Airplanes.

Biplanes left over from war training now be came the seeds of our destruction. Homemade bombs and gunfire rained down upon us. There was nowhere to run. Nowhere to hide. Black and whites were killed or injured. It didn't matter. Jealousy from those that coveted what we had took the opportunity to loot, burn and destroy. I was able to make it to Regina's family. The car was packed and we all left. There was nothing left for us here.
For any of us.

*Epilogue...*

I finally came back to greenwood for the first time. Little James said it was time to return and to bury all the feelings that we had over the years. There was also one other reason to come back.
To lay Regina to rest in the town of her birth.
As we travel along archer and greenwood, some of the buildings still remain. But not many. There are plaques lain into the sidewalks where some of the buildings once stood. Tears came to

my eyes to see the plaque where my store one stood. I was glad that Regina was not here to see this. It would have broken her heart.

They said that that only 36 people lost their lives, but others said around 300 were killed. Picked up and thrown on flatbed trucks, buried in unmarked graves. Over 1200+ buildings and businesses were burned, looted, or both. About 1.8 million in damages.
The sheriff was charged with not doing his job, but never served any time. Rowland stayed safe in jail and was taken out of town in secrecy. The charges were dropped and he never returned to Tulsa.

It's time to go home now, I made my home elsewhere, but this was a chapter in my life that I had to close. And now it's done. May those that died here rest in peace.

*The End.*

Thanks to greenwood historian Lee Alford for background information for

*Anthony Arnold*

# BLURRED LINES

My life is a blurred line
I don't know what or who I am
I don't recognize myself anymore
It is a conundrum

Society says that I am an animal
That I use violence to gain my ends
Yet I am a father, a brother, a lover
One who will support my people to no end

You can't judge a book by its cover
 And what you see may not always be
But I am told that I am less than a man
That I will never be what I should be

I try the best that I can to support family
Yet I am slapped down, pushed around
I wonder if I'm running out of time
The way I'm treated, my life is a crime

Where am I headed? Where does this life lead?
What is left for me to attain?
Will I live to see tomorrow?
Will I make it through these blurred lines?

# THE BARBER SHOP

Once upon a time, a place existed
A place where life's lessons could be learned
Where men could gather without fear of reprisal
Where young and old mingled

The barbershop

Same old men day in, and day out
Checkers and bones the game of the day
Schooling the young ones, getting a laugh or two
There is a lesson in there somewhere

The lunch lady stopping by to take the noon time orders
Catfish and hush puppies, fried chicken today
Peach cobbler or sweet potato pie for dessert
Five dollars. Hey if you don't have it I got you

The barbershop

Hey anybody seen roscoe, he haven't been here for a couple
days
Nope, but I'll go by his house right now
We looked out for each other
We were indeed family

Everyone talked trash but there was no disrespect
Especially when it came to who was the best
We young ones sat and listened
Hoping that we would be asked to share in the conversation

*Anthony Arnold*

The barbershop

They aren't the same now, no one know anyone
Used to be the same barber cut the same generations hair
Now everything is corporate, cold and unfeeling
The neighborhood shops have gone dark

I guess I long for those days to return
You see I am a product of those days
My godfather was a barber, and mine for years
I learned my life lessons from his shop

If you find one, treasure it
Sometimes just visit and listen to the elders
And maybe, just maybe
You might hear the echoes of the past

~~FINIS~~

# 24 HOURS

Only 24 hours left on this earth
I look around as I reflect on my life
Did I do all I could do for my family
And for my fellow man

Was I the father that I should have been?
Was I the husband that I needed to be?
Could I have been a better friend to those in need?
Did I live my life in accordance with his wishes?

I have tried to spread the word about our history
To let our children know from where they descended
Was there more that I could do?
Were there more that I could have reached?

As I walk down the corridor of my mind
As my time here comes to an end
I have no regrets as I go home to my reward
I watch the hours as my time comes to an end

*Anthony Arnold*

# 2013

*(The time no one cared)*

2013. Dead and gone
A hard time it was
A time when we lost ourselves
A time when no one cared

Children on the firing line
Sanford, Jacksonville. Michigan
Sandy hook
Our future taken in front of our very eyes

Stand your ground
Worked for some, not for others
You can kill an innocent teen
But not defend yourself from a DV

A child slain in front of his mother
Another in the back on the porch
A young man shot by police
Trying to help someone else

Gov't shutdown
People out of work
Tea party filibusters
Dr. Seuss is a popular read

Obamacare
Drug test for welfare
Is anyone listening?
Does anyone really care?

Benefits cut, veterans betrayed
Again those who served are f**cked
Service means nothing to some
Yet service is required

2013 was a year to be forgotten
2014 has to be better
But will anyone listen
Will anyone ever care?

*Anthony Arnold*

# A STORM IS COMING

It's out there. Can you feel it?
A storm is coming
Change is wanted, no it's needed
And it will happen

It doesn't matter who sits in the big house
Be it Black, White, Hispanic, or Asian
We are at the brink of disaster
Soon there will be no turning back

Children are being slaughtered for no reason
For loud music? Give me a break
We have more problems in this world
Other than you don't like what's on the radio

Women selling themselves for a little change
Trying to feed their kids, or their habit
More black men in prison than in college
How is our race to survive?

People can't feed their families,
Can't put a roof over their head
Congress is arguing over a tax cut for the rich
Pull your head out your ass

We are still fight a war in a place where we were never wanted
Where we were never asked to come in the first place
We've buried our sons and daughters, husbands and wives
They will be fighting long after we are gone

We can no longer continue to be the world's police man
We can't even police our own
Beatings, shootings, and corruption
What ever happened to "protect and serve?"

It's out there. Can you feel it?

A storm is coming
Change is wanted, no it's needed
And it will happen

BY ANY MEANS NECESSARY!

*Anthony Arnold*

# A SUMMER OF DISCONTENT

I fear this will be a summer of much discontent
Peace, joy and happiness will not be found
The ugly head of racism is rising again
But nothing is new about that. Is it?

Celebrities open their mouths and the venom spews
I didn't mean to use the N-word, it just happened
It just happened you say? Wow, I'm amazed
I guess slavery just happened too

People of color being slain every day
Our children, our future erased before our very eyes
Stand your ground is the new buzz phrase in use
But it's not for every one

One tracks and kills a child, but authorities refuse to act
A hoodie, ice tea and candy are the new weapons of the day
A woman fires to protect herself and her kids because of abuse
But the law doesn't apply to you. Here's your twenty years. Have a
nice day

The law says, you shall be judged by a jury of your peers
But please tell me, because I don't understand
How 6 women, ages 50-70 years old
Can be the peers of a 43 year old man?

Drugs again have raised their ugly head
Bath salts is the new meth, the new cocaine
Easy to get, addictive at the core
Drives you crazy, makes you insane

What do we do? How do we survive?
People get ready; they say the end of days is coming
For that I may respectfully disagree
I think it is already here

# AMERIKKKA

Land of the free, home of the brave
I don't think so
Dragged to our deaths
Shot without consequences

The law is blind, but only for some
Money rules the day
He who has money owns the law
Don't believe me, look around

Police brutality, modern day KKK
Thought you were to serve and protect
Not to beat and maim
No justice no peace

To be a person of color is a walking bull's eye
No matter how educated you think you are
You're looked at just the same
Just another nigga with a piece of paper

Don't worry be happy, nah I don't think so
I can't be happy when my brothers and sisters
Don't understand or don't care what's happening to them
When we are trying to be pushed back to slavery days

I can't help my people
I can't save my people
I can't warn my people
What's going on with my people?

No jobs no money, nowhere to go
Mothers can't feed their young
Men can't feed their families
Where does it end? Where does it end?

*Anthony Arnold*

# HOMELESS AND HUNGRY

I'm ashamed to beg
But I'm so hungry
Can you spare a nickel?
Or a dime?

I have nowhere to go
No place to lay my head
I do the best that I can
To live from day to day

Some days I eat, some I don't
Some days I rummage through the dumpster
Some food there is ok
It's just old

I used to have a job, a house, a family
But I fell on hard times, lost them all
So I live under an interstate
Now it's my home

So I stand here on this corner
Day in day out
Depending on the kindness of strangers
To live. To eat. To survive.

I'm ashamed to beg
But I'm so hungry
Can you spare a nickel?
Or a dime?

# HOMELESS

I see you look at me as you walk down the street
The pities on your face, the distain as you shake your head
Do you think I want to be here?
Do you think I want to be homeless?

I once was a man like you, had a job and a family
But I fell on hard times, got laid off
Lost my house, and my family
Stayed with friends, but soon was on my own

Tried to make my grind, tried to make my hustle
Got involved in drugs, couldn't keep it straight
Tried to work again, couldn't keep a job
Was never on time, didn't have a clock

My kids found me once, wanted to bring me home with them
Make me respectable they said
I wasn't a pity case, I am a man. I have pride
I left before I embarrassed them any further

So I sit here on this corner, my home now
Begging for spare change, any that you can spare
I watch the world go by, watch things change
See the young ones, lose their lives over nothing

You may see me on the corner, a little box in front
Help a brother out if you can
A nickel here, a quarter there, a dime or a penny too
I'll eat one more day, do what I must do

*Anthony Arnold*

# HOMELESS PT. 2

Walking down the streets and alleys
She walks slowly and deliberately
Her only possessions in a shopping cart
Her life, once so glamorous, reduced to shambles

If you saw her you would recognize her
She was America's sweetheart once
Before drugs, and prostitution took hold
Now she's just another homeless person

From sunup to sundown she walks
Holding conversations with herself
Business meetings that she has to get to
Her adoring fans that still want her

It was one of her fans that got her this way
Something to make you feel good he said
Take your mind off your troubles
Have you flying high

Someone recognizes her and says, hey aren't you
But she pays them no attention
Her mind is locked in a loop
Playing like a eternal movie on the screen

In a moment of clarity, she wonders how she got here
She who had everything
But her mind returns to the only reality she knows
Her ravaged body starts to walk again

As a single tear falls from her eye

# HOMELESS PT. 3

Can you help me? I just need some change to eat
I don't have anywhere to go and I'm so hungry
Anything that you can share I would be grateful for
No? Well thank you any way and god bless

I know you look at me and wonder why I'm here on the street
I can't go back home, I won't go back home
I won't let him molest me anymore
And my mother can't and won't believe me

I was nine the first time it happened
He came into my room and held me down
He took what I was supposed to give to my husband
He took my pride, he took my life

Every day until I turned 15 he came to me
Until I couldn't take it anymore
When I told my mom, she said I was lying
She said why he would want you when he has me

I left that very night and have never returned
I do what I have to do to survive
I'm not proud of the things I've done
But I did what I had to survive

I sit here now cold and alone
Wanting to turn my life around
Change, change any one? A dime or quarter
No? Well thank you any way and god bless

1.5 million= the number of children who go to sleep without a
home each year*
1 in 50= the number of children who will experience homelessness
in their lifetime*

*The National Center for Family Homelessness 2010*

*Anthony Arnold*

# LITTLE BROTHERS

It's quiet now
The firestorm has died down
But it still doesn't change a thing
My little brothers are gone

Taken before they had a chance to grow
One because of a hoodie
The other because of music
By fine up standing citizens

We don't know what they might have been
Doctor, lawyer, president
Pimp pusher criminal
But their choice was taken away

One sits in jail wondering how
The other gets himself in trouble
Yet 2 young men are gone
Sitting by the hand of the father

Little brothers you won't be forgotten
I'll keep your flames burning
I'll keep you in the safest place I know

In my heart. And in my mind.

Rest well my brothers.

# DESTINY

Is it my destiny?
To protect those gone before
To voice the voiceless
To insure they are not forgotten

Is it my destiny?
To remember injustice
To rage over our children's demise
To cry at the passing of our elders

Is it my destiny?
To remember 400+ yrs. of disrespect
To see places wiped from the map
To dine from strange fruit

Is it my destiny?
To suffer the voices I hear
Tell them, tell them they say
I do. But no one listens

Is this my destiny?
This is the question
This is my plea
This is my dilemma

Is this my destiny?

*Anthony Arnold*

# ESCAPE: A STORY OF PERSEVERANCE

*In the future.....*

I listened as I heard the slave hunters go by. "I know I saw that nigger come through here". There is no way that he could have come through here, look at that thicket, he would have to be a fool to go that way. Even the dogs won't go that way. Let's look elsewhere. As they went away from my hiding place, I breathed a sigh of relief. I removed myself from the thicket, and dabbed mud on my wounds. There was no time to rest. I had to keep moving. My life depended on it. I thought about my condition as I moved deeper into the forest. Toward freedom.

*The beginning...*

It began as I was captured in my homeland and was stolen away to this strange land across the big pond. I was taken as I carried water from the river to my village. That jug was the last thing that I will ever remember from my family and my home. My cries were silenced by a blow from a very pale man. A bright light then darkness became my world.

I awakened chained to another child in the bottom of something, I knew not what. There was moaning and crying all around me. The smell of vomit and feces ran rampant here. I called out to anyone, anyone that could help me. My voice was drowned out, for I was only a child. I made a promise that one day my voice would someday be heard.

*Part II...*

Many cycles passed on what I learned was a ship. They took us up on the top to rinse the feces and vomit off of us and to let us get sunlight. Many of us died and were thrown overboard. The waters ran red with their blood. I prayed to my god, why had he forsaken me? But I received no answer. Storms followed us as we traveled across the great water. Two ships disappeared never to be again seen. Again I prayed to my god, but I had received my answer. He had taken those two ships and allowed me to live.

*Part 3...*

Our journey finally came to an end in a strange land. We were washed and scrubbed with water from the great pond. The water burned as it got into the wounds from the chains and shackles. We were given clothes that scraped the skin and opened the sores that had scabbed over. Chained to each other, we were led to a pen where we were grouped like cattle by age and sex. We were then taken to another pen where were groped and sold to the pale men and women. I was taken along with a group of 5 other males and 3 other females. We were half marched and half dragged behind a wagon to what was to be my place of existence for the next 5 years. Until I decided that I would gain my freedom. That I would be a free man. That I would ...

ESCAPE!!!

*To be continued...*

# ESCAPE: PT. 2 – DESPERATION

It has been a year since I was brought here against my will. From my group of people, there are only me and a young girl left. The master takes her to his room every night and her screams can be heard all over the farm. Yet no one does anything about it. It is accepted. The screams remind me of the screams in my village. I cannot accept this but my time will come. Yes it will come.

*Part I...*

Working in the farm, my hands are rough and hard. I am now a muscled man, yet I am still a child. I have tasted the overseer lash and have the scars to match. As I pick this cotton and tobacco, I let my mind wonder. How can I get away from this place? I am a free man yet I am corralled like an animal. I cannot live like this. I must leave...tonight!

*Part II...*

Midnight. I slipped out of the shed that that I lived, no existed in. as I moved into the bushes into woods, I could sense freedom in my grasp. I traveled throughout the night resting during the day. I was sure that I was being followed, but I never saw anyone so I pressed on.

*Part III...*

After 5 cycles of the sun, I was sure that I had gotten away from the plantation and the hated life that I have been forced into. Not I just needed to keep going. To a new life. To freedom. I let my eyes close as I tried to rest another day.

I awoke to barking dogs, and screaming men. We got him, we got the nigger. Roughly dragged to my feet and my hands bound, I was dragged to a horse and put on its back. I was taken to a tree where there was a noose hanging down. It dawned on me that I was to be hanged. I fought with all of my being, but there were too many. I was struck on the head by one of their fire sticks. Confused, I was held up while the rope was put around my neck.

As my vision cleared, I saw the overseer looking at me with a smile on his face. This will teach you to run away, won't it? He struck the animal, who took off running. I felt the pressure around my neck as I began to swing from the rope I wondered.  Had I come so far just to die this way? Swinging from the end of a rope...?

*To be continued....*

# ESCAPE: PT. 3 - RESURRECTION

*Where am I?*

Am I dead? Have I crossed over to the land of my ancestors? The last thing I remember is the pressure around my neck as the rope tightened. I gasped as the air could no longer reach my chest. I saw my family as consciousness seeped away from my mind. A shock of pain and then...Nothing.

*Part I...*

My eyes fluttered open, yet I could not see. I was in total darkness all around. I dared not call out, as I did not know where I was. A groan escaped my lips as I tried to move around. Ah, you're awake. We wondered if we had reached you in time. Relax and rest. Your throat is bruised and you won't be able to talk for a while. Here is some cool water. Drink slowly and rest. It hurt to swallow, but I did as the person said. Slowly I felt sleep overcome me. I welcomed it with open arms.

*Part II...*

I awoke again to see a stern woman sitting next to me. Who are you? Where am I? I said in a rough voice. I rubbed my throat and felt the scar of the rope around my neck. The woman watched as I rubbed the scar around my neck. She finally said that is a reminder of how close you came to death. Remember it well she said, as she walked out of the room.

*Part III...*

I did not see the woman for a couple of day while I gathered my strength. My voice had become raspy, and I was told that it would never change. She handed me a scarf and said wear this if you wish for people not to stare. I looked around and asked where am i. you are at a station on the Underground Railroad. We help slaves to escape. At the look on my face she smiled and said there is no train, but there is a route. Who are you I asked as she turned left to leave the room.

She turned and with a solemn look said, I am Harriet Tubman and I am your best hope of survival.

*To be continued...*

# ESCAPE: PT 4 - REDEMPTION

"I am Harriet Tubman and I am your best hope of survival." Her eyes pierced into mine as she stared into my face. I felt my soul open as she spoke to me, but I never heard her words. All I could focus on was her eyes. Burning. Burning. Burning.

*Part I...*

I stayed with Miss Tubman and the railroad for a week. Traveling by night, hiding by day. There were even the pale ones who helped us by getting us food and clothing. But I felt that I could not stay with them for much longer. I needed to be on my own. I needed to be free.

*Part II...*

I told Miss Tubman of my wish and even though she did not agree with me, she wished me well. So with a small package of clothing and food, I gave my farewell and moved off into the forest. After the company the past week, I never felt more alone. I heard voices everywhere I went. Sleep was hard to come by. I kept seeing the rope going around my neck, and the pressure as it tightened around my neck. I always came awake as I fell off the animal as the rope tightened. Dogs I heard barking, men I heard yelling in the distance. My mind was not my own anymore

Mungu ila Mimi. God save me.

*Part III...*

I awoke as a cool breeze blew across my body. I was covered with sweat. I reached up and felt the scar around my neck. Yes this has been no dream. It had all been real. I needed to find cover. I had been lying out in the open, yet I had not been discovered. The gods had indeed been looking over me. I went to find shelter, to hide until the safety of the night.

*Epilogue...*

I made it to the north after two more months. I was taken in by a couple and taught to be a blacksmith, where I still work until this day. My dream of being a free man became a reality. I sometimes wonder what became of those who journeyed from the homeland with me. Were they as lucky as I was or did they die a shameful death in a land that was not their own.

Harriett Tubman and the Underground Railroad freed by some estimates 100,000 slaves over the time span of the railroad. Even though this is a fictional account, who is to say that it didn't happen?

*The End*

*Anthony Arnold*

# MANDELA

In a South African hospital lies a man
No not just a man, a symbol of freedom
Of determination, of justice and peace
His name is Nelson Mandela

The heartbeat of a country
The soul of his people
A symbol of persistence
A hammer of resistance

Imprisoned for most of his life
Apartheids worst enemy
His faith would not falter
His strength would not wane

He is the lifeblood of the people
The leader of the new day
A king who has regained his throne
Yet humble and quiet

He comes now to the end
Dignity still radiates from his soul
He prepares for his homecoming
To walk along the glory road

Martin, Malcolm, and Gandhi
Stand and await him
He will be welcomed
He will be at home.

uthi, Makwandiswe kuni inceba noxolo nothando
Mercy unto you, and peace, and love, be multiplied
These things I wish upon you
Nelson Rolihlahla Mandela

In honor of Mr. Mandela, who transitioned to the land of the ancestors at the age of 95'

*Anthony Arnold*

# OUR HISTORY

Kidnapped from our lands
Beaten, enslaved
Sold like animals
This is our history

Men, women and children taken
Families erased, bloodlines diminished
Split apart, never to be seen again
This is our history

Fire hoses, dogs
Protests, and marches
Nooses and shallow graves
This is our history

Come forward today
Babies having babies
Our people disrespecting our people
This is our present

Pimps pushin, drugs dealing
Pants sagging, children dying
Black on black crime
This is our present

They say what goes around comes around
Well that skipped us
We're caught in a vicious circle
Those who don't know their history

Are doomed to repeat it
This is our present

This is our history

#breakthecircle

# REFLECTIONS

As I sit and listen the rain
The tears flow down my face
Hurt and pain grip my heart
Thinking about my own history

I watched my gram and great gram work in the fields
Toiling from sunup to sundown
Just to provide for me
Just so I wouldn't have to

I think back to the small town I grew up in
The struggle of being a small fish in a big pond
Watching crosses burn and people die
Not knowing what my future would hold

The things that I endured as a child
Help me grow as a man
But in times like these
I can still see their face

That's why I burn with our history
Why I try to spread our past
Our children must know where we come from
Sacrifices made for their behalf

I would like to think that they would be proud of me
To think that I finally made something of myself
Well gram and great gram I do this to honor you
To honor the sacrifice that you made for me.

Thank you. I love you. I miss you.

*Anthony Arnold*

# REFLECTIONS PT 2

I sit here, stared at, and lusted by you
But you don't see what I see
I see a princess, a queen
All you see is a slut, a whore

Raised to honor my man, my king
To perpetrate my race
To you all I am is a piece of meat
Something to sex and throw away

I am the color of mocha
Able to melt in your mouth
But to you I am an aberration
Nothing better than dirt

You gaze and lust for
My full breasts, my wide hips
But you would rape and slaughter me
Without a single thought

I see the worth in my man my king
The power in his words, his life
You hang him from trees
Take away his manhood

I am a black woman
Prideful, loving, and strong
But all you see is a reflection
Someone who fades away.

# REFLECTIONS 3:

*(Inside a Racist Mind)*

Looking in this mirror, I don't see me
I see who I used to be
Young and strong, able to do anything
Not as I am now old and feeble

I relish the choices I made
The things I did
I did as I was taught by my pappy and his pappy
It was my right

I'm fourth generation Klansman, born and bred
My father and his father, and his father's father
This was what we did, and still do
The family business I guess

It was our right to burn the cross in that yard
To watch them run with nothing but the clothes on their back
To hold the father, while we raped and slaughter the wife
To lynch the father while their child watched

Amerikka is for the righteous is our cry
Shooting a young interracial couple on their night out
Theirs bodies never to be found
Mixing of the races, not allowed

Marching at the front of the parade, 100 strong
Feeling the hate from the monkeys, the Jews, the spics
None of you belong here
This is our land.

I was right to look into the eyes of the victim
To relish the fear radiating from his body
Help me he said, I have a family, don't kill me
So I helped him. Right into a grave

*Anthony Arnold*

I look into my life, knowing I was just. Knowing I right.
Of course I was right. I have god on my side
We are the chosen ones.
We will prevail.

A different look. From the other side.

# ROSEWOOD

Time stands still here
Listen and you will hear the screams
Look and you will see the carnage
People dying, buildings burned.

Was she or wasn't she?
No one knows for sure the answer
A drifter, black of course
Took her flower, a maiden of the south

Vigilante justice any justice must be served
Get those niggas get them all
Lynch him! Was he even the right one?
It didn't matter. He was black. He was the right one

Blacks didn't take it, they fought back
Heroic, yet futile gestures
Oh we can't have this
Burn it. Burn it all to the ground

Run! Run! Everyone save yourselves
Take yo families hide
To the swamps we go
Wait until it is safe

Six blacks were killed, along with two whites
And a town erased from the map
No one was charged, no one cared
Blacks left and never returned

Time stands still here
Listen and you will hear the screams
Look and you will see the carnage
People dying, buildings burned

*Anthony Arnold*

# SEGREGATION

Separate but equal
The biggest fallacy ever committed
How can this be?
Why was this allowed?

Our children, slaves to the system
Learning the best that they could
Hand me down books
Buildings unsafe, even for the rats

Separate but equal
Jim Crow at its finest
Separate water fountains
Dining rooms out back

Were we not all made in god's image?
Where does it say white's here?
All others over there
Please show me...don't worry I'll wait

We were even segregated according to skin color
Lighter skinned looked down on our darker brethren
Did you think you could progress by living a lie?
By setting aside who you were, a person of color

My heart aches and my eyes tear, thinking of injustice
Lain upon us, forced upon us
Our people did not ask to be brought here
But I will be damned if I will be treated less than the man I am

Our children will never have to go through what I did
The heartbreak of being told you can't come in here
You can't go over there
All because of the color of their skin

# A CONVERSATION

Hello my name is Tony
I've seen you around
And this I had to tell you
But I don't want you to take this wrong

I've noticed the way that you carry yourself
And I must admit it has me quite intrigued
Quiet elegance, beauty and intelligence
I like what I see

Now I would like to get to know you
And I'm not just spitting a line
I would just like to get the chance to
See what you're about

Name the time and name the place
I'm in no rush, some things you cannot
Put a time frame on
Let me learn you at your leisure

Dinner and dancing, in public if you wish
But I am an accomplished cook
Let me share this with you
Let me do this for you

I didn't mean to interrupt
And I know you have many men
Who would like to be close to you
This was something I had to say
Hope that you don't mind

Enjoy your day
And thank you for your time
My name is Tony
And I've seen you around

*Anthony Arnold*

# DO YOU LIKE THE RAIN?

She watched the old man gaze out the window
Staring at the rain as he always did
She decided to ask him why he always did
Excuse me, do you like the rain

He slowly turned to look into her face
She could see the tears well up in his eyes
I'm sorry did I say something wrong
I just wanted to know why you stare into the rain

In a quiet voice so low she could barely hear it
The rain reminds me of my sweet, sweet wife
My flower, my heart
She left on a day such as this

I never thought that she would be the one to go first
I was the one who raised all the hell, took all the chances
She was the quiet one, the one who laughed at my jokes
Helped me up when I fell, was my rock when I faltered

We used to sit when it rained and watch it pour
She said when it rained the angels were crying
But their tears helped everything grow
To make the flowers bloom

One rainy day she said she wasn't feeling well
And to the doctor we went
He told me that she had known she was sick
But she didn't want me to worry

She told me that it was time for her to go home
to bloom in God's garden
But don't worry I'll see you again some day
I'll watch over you from his garden

So now you know why I stare at the rain

My wife still watches over me from god's garden
Letting me know she still is in bloom
That she is still watching over me

A year later, on a rainy day he passed in his sleep
She could only let her tears flow as she smiled
For she could see him next to his wife his beloved flower
As they both bloomed in god's garden

*Anthony Arnold*

# LOVE JONES

I sit here with my heart in my hands
I don't understand this feeling that surrounds me
This glow that I feel whenever I hear your name
Whenever I see your face

I knew from the minute that I saw you
My heart would never be mine again
That my life would never be empty
That I would share my love forever

I find myself waiting to hear your voice
Over the distance, over the miles
Just for a little while
My heart beats just a little faster, a little stronger

Right now this house is not a home
Because you're not here
But our love will survive
It is too strong not to be

I was blessed when God brought you into my life
I didn't know what I had done to deserve you
But I promise that I will love, cherish and honor
These things for you I will do

Let me be your rock, your shelter in a storm
When your cold, let me keep you warm
When you're sad, my shoulder you can cry on
When you need, let me be the one to give

I'll be here whenever you may need
My heart for you I'll bleed
Blessed I am from up above
With you I'll always share my love

# ROSES AND BARBED WIRE

She said that her heart was a rose in barbed wire
Closed off from the world
She couldn't take the pain and the sorrow
Love for her was no longer a reality

She said she gave her all to her man
Would do anything, would go anywhere
Ride or die, this was who she was
He threw it all back in her face

So she raised the wall around herself
Placed the barbed wire around her rose
Never again will I love
Never again

Don't close yourself off I said
Love will come when you least expect it
There is some one for you
There is some one for everyone

How can you be sure, how do you know
Because I too was once like you
Closed off and withdrawn from the world
Thinking I would never love again

She found me, and showed me that love was possible
That's how I know that it will happen for you
Give it a chance and you too will find the love you seek
The love that you desire, the love you cherish

She said that her heart was a rose in barbed wire
Closed off from the world
She said she would give it another try
To find love once again

# SELF LOVE: AN EROTIC SHORT STORY

She gazes upon herself in the mirror. Not bad she thinks. Breasts firm, flat stomach, and a tight ass. Her hands flow over her body. Her breasts begin to ache, her nipples rising. She feels that familiar longing in the pit of her stomach. Her body craves release. It craves satisfaction.

Slowly walking to her bed, she thinks about her lover. Her passion starts to flow as she thinks about him ravishing her. But no, not tonight.

*Tonight is all about her.*

Lying on her bed, she lets her mind take control. She imagines his touch as he slowly kisses his way along her body. Her breath quickens as she feels his lips caress her breasts. She sighs and shakes as she feels his tongue tracing the route to her forbidden fruit.

Her hands tease her body as her imagination runs wild. She feels the object of her desire as it rises from its hiding place begging to be touched. Her fingers slowly caress it, covering it with her love juices. She imagines his lips fastening themselves around it as he flicks it with his tongue. Her body shakes with her first orgasm as she rubs slowly. Gently.

Her juices flow into a puddle on the bed, but she doesn't care. Her body is covered with sweat. Her moans echo in the silence of the room. There is nothing but her.

*And him.*

She feels herself heading to the point of no return. She pulls her legs up and slides a finger deep inside her wetness. She gasps as her vagina grasps it. She imagines him entering her, deeply slowly. Her body shakes with each thrust. She cries out as she brings herself time and time to the edge, only to let herself fall away.

Finally her body betrays her. Orgasm after orgasm ravishes her. No! No! She cries out but she is too far gone. Her body shakes until she is spent.

There is nothing but the sound of her shallow breathing. A single tear runs down her face. A small smile and maybe a telephone call.

*Maybe.*

~~FINI~~

*Anthony Arnold*

# TASTY

Staring at your body after we make love
I trace the sweat that runs between your breasts
The look in your eyes
Silently asking for more

I long to taste your body
I kiss my way down your body
Licking every curve
Savoring every part of you

Finding your flower I want to make it bloom
I kiss, caress, lick and nibble it
You legs tighten and pull me in closer
Deeper and deeper I go

Tangy and sweet, you are to me
Your scent arouses me
I hear you moaning
As your hands pull me in.

You start to shake as you erupt
I break away and slowly enter as you cum
Your breath catches as you slip over the edge
And you tighten around me

I taste you again as I drink all of you
As you give me all of you
Tangy and sweet

Tasty

# THE 5 TENETS OF LOVE

Have you wondered why relationships last?
And some never got past first base
There are certain things that need to be done
I call them the 5 tenets of love

**Communication**

You have to be able to communicate with your mate
To listen, and understand what he or she is telling you
Sometimes it's not what they are saying; it's what they're not
It can make all the difference in the world

**Affection**

Show a little affection to your mate from time to time
It doesn't have to be a big production, something simple will do
A flower, a kiss, sometimes just a hug will do
Just as long as they know that you care, the difference will be made

**Caring**

This may seem the same as affection, but is a little bit different
A kiss at the door, a hot bath, a glass of wine
Dinner waiting, maybe a massage
Which will lead into this

**Love**

I say love instead of sex, because now is the time for foreplay
Explore your mate's body, learn and re-learn what makes them melt
Make this time erotic; take your time no need to rush
Help them fall in love all over again

*Anthony Arnold*

**I love you**

Three simple words that are never said enough
Three words that can brighten their day
Let them know that you will be there for them
Come rain or shine, you will be their back bone, their strength

These are not the end all to be all
You know what will work for you and yours
Love and treasure your mate
You may never get this chance again

# THE JAZZ SINGER

Let me sing and play for you
Let my music say everything that I cannot
I'm just a jazz singer, a man with a mission
Let me make you fall in love

Let my music raise your passion
Lifting you up to let your emotions soar
Lowering you down gently and softly
Making your heart beat once again

I sing to tell you what I dare not say
A glimpse of the emotion that I have inside
I sing the things that I carry in my heart
Over and over again

From smoky bars to large arenas
From festivals, to command performances
I sing my songs of love
I sing them all for you

No one knows the pain that I feel
I hide the things that I feel inside
Knowing that the song that I sing
Is a feeling that I will never know

So I sing for you, feelings that I will never know
To get you to fall in love once again
Letting my music do for you what I cannot
I'm just a jazz singer

*Anthony Arnold*

# WEDDING DAY

It was supposed to be the happiest day of his life
So why didn't it feel that way?
Why did it feel that something was missing?
Why did if feel wrong?

Thinking back to other times
The woman that he loved, the one who carried his heart
No longer loved him, no longer cared
The one he lost because he couldn't keep his junk in his pants

Now it has come to this, a moment that will affect him for the rest
of his life
A woman who he has professed to love waiting on the other side
A church full of friends and relatives waiting
His one true love not there

The best man came out of the back of the church with a note in his
hand
He walked over and gave it to the father of the bride
He read it and gave it to the pastor
For reasons known only to the groom, there will be no wedding on
this day

He felt lighter than he had ever felt. He was sorry but he knew she
would understand
Theirs was not to be a marriage of love, only convenience
Now he had to find the one who was the woman of his dreams
Now he had to find ...Her

# WEDDING DAY PT. 2

She sat listening to what used to be their favorite song
Crying, being angry, and crying again
He's getting married now and there is nothing I can do
Why did I let him go? Why?

The memories began to flow back to the beginning
His smile, his laugh, the way he spoke her name
The way she felt when he touched her
The way she called out when he made love to her

She remembered that fateful day when her best friend
Called and told her he had made love to her
Her sense of betrayal and shame. The hurt she felt.
She sent him away with a text, she couldn't face him

Over the months he tried to tell her what happened
She refused to speak with him, to let him speak
Until one day he stopped trying, no calls and no text
Until she heard that the two of them were getting married

Good riddance she thought. They deserve each other
I can do bad all by my self
But as the days got closer, she began to regret her decision
Until the time got too late

As the clock struck three, the dagger pieced her heart
He is hers now, nothing I can do. The doorbell rang
And as she opened the door, her heart began to sing
He stood at her door. But why?

*Anthony Arnold*

# WEDDING DAY PT. 3

As she opened the door her heart leapt into her throat
Her mouth moved but no sound came out
Aren't you going to say something? Anything?
Why aren't you married?

I couldn't do it, he said as he walked into her apartment
It wasn't going to be right; I had to see you to explain
There is nothing to explain she said, tears welling up
You slept with her, that is all there is to it

You say that, she says that. The thing is I don't remember it
What do you mean you don't remember it? Is she that bad?
No I don't remember it at all. NOTHING AT ALL!!!
Tell me what you do remember she said

I went there because I needed her help to surprise you
I was going to propose to you and I wanted her help
Her eyes got wide as she listened to him explain
Could she have possibly been wrong about all of this?

She told me to come over to her house and we could talk there
When I got there she had dinner and wine ready
We talked and drank the wine. I didn't feel that I could drive
And she said I could crash on her couch

The next morning I woke up naked on her couch with her
Draped all around me. She said I was an excellent lover
The next thing I knew she had called you and said we slept
together
This brings us to where we are now

I understand if you don't want me, but I had to tell you my side
But I'm not going to go back to her. I don't love her I love you!
As he got up to leave she reached for his hand and softly said
Stay with me. Don't go...Don't go...

Nine months later

Isn't she beautiful? He said as he held his newborn daughter
Yes she is, she said. What do you want to name her?
Let's name her Hope. That's what I feel every time I look at you
He pulled out a ring and slid it on to her hand and said

Will you marry me?

Yes!

*Anthony Arnold*

# WHAT IS LOVE?

What is love? Is it happy ever after?
Is it rainbows and finding your prince charming?
Is it finding the woman of your dreams?
Maybe. Maybe not

Love is hard work, not always peaches and cream.
It is blood, sweat and tears. Mostly tears.
It's coming home and having to tell your mate you
Lost your job when you are already a month behind

It's having to put up with in-laws that you know don't like you
But you do it for them because you know it would break their heart
If you spoke your mind

Love is eating a dish that you mate spent all day cooking
Even though it not worth eating you do it anyway
And tell them it was the best thing you ever had

It's having their back through thick and thin
Sometimes against conventional wisdom
Not saying I told you so if they fail
And not gloating too much when they succeed

Love is sometimes agreeing to disagree
Being the big enough person to admit when you're wrong
And being a bigger enough person not to rub it in when you're
right

For me, it's waking up to stare into your eyes in the morning
To hear your voice just saying hi I'm here
To surprise you with your favorite dinner, to have a bath waiting
for you

That's what love is to me

# A VETERAN'S SORROW

I watch the news and I see the celebration
The troops are coming home
Ticker tape and parades
I say, good for them

But not long ago I came home too
Where was my ticker tape?
My welcome home
Where was my parade?

I came home to scorn and ridicule
Go back to where you came from baby killer
Spit upon, cursed at, disowned
Why? I followed the orders from those above me

I came home to empty airports
Where people pulled their kids away
Like I was some kind of monster
Like I had done something wrong

I fought from the age of seventeen
So they could do those very things
To disrespect me and those
Who didn't come back with me.

The friends and compatriots
That I hear in my head
That I will hear
For the rest of my life

MEDIC! MEDIC! Won't this ever stop?
Friends dying, disfigured
Screams and more screams
Lord please make it stop

I live from day to day, week to week

*Anthony Arnold*

The government says im disabled
They say I have PTSD
I say I miss my friends

So I watch the TV, and follow the war
Watch the kids as they come home
Some maimed, some whole, some in bags
But as least they come home
I am glad that America honors their heroes
Their warriors, their best
Maybe one day they will honor us
Maybe then the voices inside me will rest

To all Vietnam veterans, I salute you
Air Force Gulf war, Iraqi and Enduring Freedom
Veteran, 1986-2009

# A VETERAN'S STORY

I see the look in your eyes
The distaste as you walk away
I hear the words that you mutter
Dirty individual, get a job

I'm not here because I want to be
I'm here because of circumstance
I'm here because of the voices in my head
Because of the faces that I see in my sleep

I am the reason you can drive your fine car
Wear your fancy clothes
I am the reason we are not speaking Japanese
I am a Veteran. A homeless veteran

I ran on the beaches at Normandy
Helped raise the flag at Iwo Jima
Sludge thru the muck in Vietnam
Crossed the deserts of Iraq

Some came home to boos and jeers
Others came home to parades and cheers
Some came home in boxes and less than whole
Some never came home at all

No man likes to beg
Everyone deserves a roof over their head
A hot meal once and a while
A place to call home

There are 57,000 of my brothers on the street
We do the best we can
Sometimes we make it
Sometimes the streets become our tomb

So just remember the next time before you speak

*Anthony Arnold*

Before you ridicule or mock the one on the street
He or she is a veteran, worthy of respect
And was willing to give their life for you

MSgt (ret) Anthony Arnold
USAF 1986-2009

# BULLIED

My life is trial
Every day I fear for my life
Why you ask?
Because I am bullied

It started back in elementary school
First it was toys, then lunch money
Books torn, clothes taken
Life a living hell

I run home, take different ways
Tell my parents, tell the principal
None of it helps
None of it helps

Bruises, bones broken
Nothing can be done
No witnesses
None that will talk anyway

Down to my last straw
Can't take this anymore
They won't stop it
I will, I will

Here he comes
Not this time
This stops now
No more

I pull out the piece
No more
No more bullying
Not now, now ever

Why you crying

*Anthony Arnold*

Why you begging
You the big man
Be bad now

Who's the bitch now?
Huh? Who's the bitch now?
Damn. Did you just piss on yourself?

I gave them the gun
It wasn't even real
He didn't know that

Everyone looks at me funny
Says I finally snapped
Maybe so
But I'm not bullied anymore

HAHAHAHAHAHAHA!

# DON'T CARE ANY MO'

Say what you want to me
Do what you think you can
Jealousy and rage doesn't affect me
Don't care any mo'

Im blessed from a higher power
And walk on a higher plane
You can't see me
Don't care any mo'

Until you walk in my shoes
Know the passion in my heart
Until you act like a grown man
Don't care any mo'

I am among many
A guardian for my people
A teacher of our history
A preacher of truth

You may silence my voice
But my words will live on
My passion will burn
You I don't fear

Raise your head and see my people
Lower your head and hear our footsteps
You'll see me; I'll be right out front
Cause I don't care any mo'

*Anthony Arnold*

# DRED SCOTT

I am a man, created by my father
Brought to life in his image
From him all men are free
How can you tell me this cannot be?

All men are free in the eyes of the father
Your laws do not hold sway over me
Yet you tell me I am a slave
Freedom I have, freedom I will crave

The places I've lived, places that been
Even my current "master" says it is wrong
So who are you to tell me that I am not a free man?
Is this part of your master plan?

The courts in Missouri said that I and my wife should be free
That we had been held illegally
But other courts said that no you should not
You will be a slave until you die and rot

How can this be? Am I not a man?
Does you law no mean anything
Is it just something to be discarded when you wish
Empty words to placate those who would ask?

I shall not waver; I will not stop this challenge
Our lives are our own, dictated by no one
I will succeed and I will win
For I am a man, I am no one's slave

On March 6, 1857, The United States Supreme Court ruled
that no slave free or otherwise, could be considered a citizen
Of the United States. A decision that helped push the country to
Civil war.

# HOLLOW DREAMS

My life is hollow now without you
There is a hole in my heart
Where your love used to be
The tears that flow now that we are apart

My arms long to hold you
My lips long to kiss you
I feel hollow without you
This bed will never be the same

The things that I feel I can't express
Maybe that's why you left
But if I could tell you the things that are in my heart
Would you come back to me?

I feel a weight upon my chest that won't allow me to breathe
A heaviness that won't go away
The love that I feel for you continues to grow
Tell me if we still will be together

Come back to me, come back home
I don't care if I have to walk, crawl
This feeling that I have, I know
My heart is numb, my soul is hollow

*Anthony Arnold*

# LEGACY

*(Is this how it ends)*

Somewhere in the Pacific,

Crouched in this foxhole
Bullets flying by my head
Screams of medic pierce the air
The smell of death and fear linger

I wonder if I'm next, could my time be up
Fighting here on a rock, cause I'm told to
GRENADE! Someone yells
as I jump on it I wonder

Is this how it ends?

Somewhere in the skies of SW Asia

I fly again over this god forsaken land
Bombing another forest, hoping I get lucky
Trying to bring this beast home
So that I can get back home

Many have perished, never to be seen again
Or reside in the grand Hanoi Hilton
Beaten and paraded like cattle
Pawns in a war not of our making

BOOM!!!! WE'RE HIT, EJECT, EJECT!!
Everyone goes, I'm last out
I pull my handle. Nothing happens
As she rolls over I wonder

Is this how it ends?

In the deserts of Kuwait

Riding patrol on the highway of death
Trying to stay alert
Trying to do my job
It's quiet now, not as it was

Tanks, bombs exploding, people dying
Chaos, destruction everywhere
Nothing left, bodies and scrap metal
Left to rust. Left to die

I see it all in my mind
I never heard the call
IED, IED they said
As the concussion lifts the Humvee

I wonder

Is this how it ends?

In a classified location somewhere in the Arctic Ocean

XO, I have the con
Yes Ma'am, captain has the con
Never thought I would hear those words
Much less say them

First in my class at the academy
First woman selected for submarine duty
First to command a ballistic missile boat
Now maybe the first to fire a nuke in anger

Message is confirmed authentic from command authority
Oh god! WW3 has begun. Got to do my job
Very well, open doors one and two
Get ready to fire on my command

Come to missile firing depth
As we rise, wonder what the rest of my family would say
They gave their lives in battle

*Anthony Arnold*

Guess it's my turn now

Firing depth reached. Very well
Torpedo in the water. 1000 yards
Thank you. Keep her steady
Fire on my mark.

It has been an honor to serve with all of you.

5-600 yards and closing
4-500 yards and closing
3-400 yards and closing
2-300 yards and closing
200 yards and closing

FIRE!

100 yards

Is this how it ends?

BOOOOOOOOM!

# ON THE CHAIN GANG

It's hot out here on this road
Working on this here chain gang
Boss watching to make sure I don't run
Shotgun in hand to blast a nigga

Got 20 to life for killin this fool
I'm innocent I said, but it didn't matter
I was black, he was white
In the south, that don't go

You ride by in your fancy car
Turn your nose up at me
I just laugh and shake my head
If I was close you would mess yourself

Yes suh boss I'm movin
Breakin these rocks to make this road
Somethin I'll never travel
Except on this prison bus

Every day in this hot sun
We work with a little bit of water
A slice of bread and some meat
Drop dead no one cares

Yes suh boss I'm movin
Breaking the rocks
Daydream here and there
Working on this here chain gang

*Anthony Arnold*

# PAIN

Pain comes in many ways
But the pain that I fell cannot be described in one measure
My heart feels squeezed my soul buried
Physically drained, mentally done

There has to be a way to end what I feel
Some ways are not an option even though maybe quick
Then I would push my pain to someone else
That I would not and will not do

I can only fall to my knees and ask you
Lord please hear my call
I know not what to say or do
I can only ask you to help me through this pain

I am not a religious person per say
But I know you are there I humbly submit myself to you
The tears flow freely from mine eyes
The only thing I know left to do

Lord I ask that you help me in my pain
That you help me to be strong
Help me to walk in your path
Help me is all that I can ask

A charge to keep I have
A god to glorify
A never-dying soul to save
And fit it for the sky

# PAIN PT. 2

This pain I feel inside
The tears that I cry
These I shed for my people
For you and I

Where have we done to think?
That all will be handed to us on a platter
That we can do whatever we want
That the consequences won't matter

Look at ourselves in the mirror
Search inside our souls
Have we done everything that we could?
Have we walked the line, let our emotion grow cold

The things that I see, I can only shake my head
Losing our youth, killing ourselves dead
Where are the elders to show them the way
To teach them that there is a brighter day

We as the old hats have been remiss
Our duty to the young ones we have let slip
Someone else will do it, we've said
We got to get up ourselves and get a grip

We can't sit back and pass it on to someone else
We have to go and step into the fire
Preach to the young ones
Even though it may raise the ire

Think back to the time you sat at the knee
The words that were passed on to you
Now it is you that are the one to speak
As you sit under that wisdom tree

*Anthony Arnold*

# REJOICE

We rejoice in ourselves and family
We survive the pain and hardships
Being captured and brought from our ancestral home
Treated more as an animal than human

We rejoice in our father, our god almightily
Who delivered us from Egypt
From the hands of pharaoh
Between the parted red sea

We rejoice our heritage, those from which we came
Kings and queens, royalty beyond compare
We are those who will transcend
Those who will overcome

We rejoice the heart of our people
The strength of our people
Resilience and power of our people
The love of our people

We who have come after
Must rejoice in our hearts
Think with our minds
Rejoice in all that we do

He will put no more that we can stand
In our darkest hour, in our time of need
Our ancestors will answer our call
And our souls will...

REJOICE!

# REVENGE

I sit here on this dark cold floor
His blood drips from the knife in my hand
I told him karma is a bitch
Revenge is a dish best served cold!

It started when I was 10
He said it was just a game between me and him
That no one needed to know
That he was my lover now

The pain, so intense, I blacked out
I thought it was a dream
But I awoke to a nightmare
Blood everywhere

Over the years it continued
Every night, 10 on the dot
When my mother goes to work
Into my room he comes

I've found another place to go
I let my mind wander
I barely hear his grunts and groans
Barely

No one believed me when I told
My mother didn't believe me
I was dreaming they said
There was no way

Day by day I formed a plan
I would get my freedom
He would never have me again
He would never rape me again

I waited until we were alone

*Anthony Arnold*

Until he was sated and weak
And as he started to sleep
I drove the knife into his chest

Blood gushed as I stabbed him
Again. Again and again
Until he drowned in his own blood
Until he could breathe no more
I sit here now awaiting the police
This knife in my hand
I told him karma is a bitch
Revenge is a dish best served cold!

# SHIPS IN THE NIGHT

Two people floating in a sea of loneliness
Never knowing, never feeling that love was near
Passing each other like ships in the night
Never knowing love's safe harbor

Found by love's warming light
Hearts and lives intertwined
Wanting no more than to live and love
To share in what life has in store

He is her protector, her lover, her light in a storm
She is his heart, his strength, his life
Together they will live life as one
What god has put together, let no man tear asunder

*Anthony Arnold*

# STRANGE FRUIT

*(Inspired by the song by Billie Holiday)*

Strange fruit she said, hanging from the branch of the poplar tree
Yet this is not the south, this is Indiana
Two men, their lives taken violently
Slain by a lynch mob, justice denied

Accused of rape and murder, no justice would be seen
Broken out of jail, beaten and lynched
But this isn't the south these are civilized folk
We are still just niggers to them

Hung from the tree, life's struggle begun
One lowered, arms broken and hung again
Even though the victim say she was not raped
Vigilante justice will prevail

Judge, jury and executioner all in one
Two less Pick-a-ninnies to deal with
Our civic duty is done, protected our folk
Let's go get a beer. How's the family?

Two men beaten and hanging from a tree
Silent testament to the violence of the times
No justice no peace
Strange fruit indeed

Thomas Shipp and Abram Smith
Not lynched in the south
But in Indiana
Nowhere is safe, nowhere

# SURVIVAL

Somewhere on the plains of Malawi
A child wonders his fate
Will he live to see manhood?
Or will he join his ancestors

Food is scarce
Water even more so
Yet he solders on
By force of indomitable will

His playmates disappear
Funeral pyres grow
Mass graves abound
Mothers wail

He takes his small portion
And takes what nourishment he can
Pondering his fate
Wondering his destiny

Somewhere a child survives
His life a chance
Will he continue on this path?
Or close his eyes for the last time

*Anthony Arnold*

# THE BOOK OF POETRY

On a mountaintop in a land faraway
Guarded by global wordsmiths
The power behind all poets and poetesses
The book of poetry

Inside this book lies the wisdom of the ages
Poetry from the beginning of time
Our hearts bleeds from this book
Our souls are contained in this book

Langston Hughes, Maya Angelou
Nikki Giovanni, Paul Laurence Dunbar
Our muses, our inspiration
Our power

We all aspire to be included in this book
To be the inspiration for generations to come
To be the ones that they look up to
The ones that are shared among the masses

On a mountaintop in a land faraway
Guarded by global wordsmiths
The power behind all poets and poetesses
The eternal book of poetry

# THEY DON'T CARE ABOUT US

*(Inspired by Michael Jackson)*

They don't care about us
People dying in the streets
Not enough food to eat
Shut yo mouths take your seat

They don't care bout us

Children gone, lives taken
Stand your ground, bull shit just fakin
Signing autographs, money making
Karma's coming one day you won't be wakin

They don't care bout us

Homeless abound, no end in sight
Veterans on the street, nah this aint right
Whole families in a box, looking for light
When do we end this, stop the endless slight?

They don't care bout us

No pride in ourselves, our enemies we are
Will we ever learn, does anyone care
What would martin, would Malcolm say
We've lost our muse, we've lost our way

We don't care about us

Airplane vanished, in a clear blue day
Help us find it, we don't know the way
I hope and pray that they all went to heaven
Cause aliens can't carry a 777

They might care about them

*Anthony Arnold*

# UNTITLED #6

Alone here I sit
My mind far away
My heart is heavy
My soul is forlorn

Love eludes me
Am I not worthy of its bliss?
What have I done wrong?
Has karma found its vengeance?

I have not always been the best
But I've tried to do what is right
But as I get older, the thing that I crave the most
Is the thing that I cannot find?

Companionship, love and passion
Are these things not meant for me?
Holding hands, long walks
Things I cannot see

Have I not been a good man with those I've shared a life
A good provider, a kind lover
A man who puts his other before himself
These things I don't understand

Maybe I am only to write about it, not experience it
To watch it blossom for others, yet wilt in my hand
To remember past loves, yet experience nothing new
To walk my path alone

I shall not be bitter; my heart will not grow hard
I will celebrate in the glow of my friends
But when I am alone at night in solitude
Mine eyes will shed a tear

# UNTITLED 14

My sister, what has happened?
I see you hanging from the tree of woe
Taken away before your time
I weep for you my sister

Beaten, raped and hung
Because you would not succumb
To racists who hide themselves
Under a Christian guise

Giving your life to save your man
To further the cause
Yet treated as nothing more than trash
To be taken out and discarded

Tears of anger flow down my face
As I see you swing lightly in the breeze
A mother, sister, daughter or wife
Gone from among us

My sister, what has happened?
I see you hanging from the tree of woe
Taken away before your time
I weep for you my sister

*Anthony Arnold*

# VIOLATED

I have been violated

Whipped, beaten. Taken
Manhood removed
No longer considered human
Shackled, lynched

I feel violated

Segregated, you can't sit here
Not allowed there
Sit-ins a must
Jim Crow not the norm

We are violated

I have a dream, by any means necessary
March for our rights
Fight if we must
Die if need be

Flaming busses, attacked by dogs
Water hoses, jail cells
Shallow graves
Bodies never found

Our children are violated

The bull's eye is on their backs
Slaughtered before our eyes
Emmitt Till, four young ladies
Trayvon martin, Jordan Davis

My rights are violated

Profiled, driving while black

Wearing a hoodie
You can't own that car
You can't live in this neighborhood

Where do we go?
What do we do?
When will we be able?
Not to feel

Violated

*Anthony Arnold*

# VOICES

I hear the voices in my head
Friends, family, compatriots
Please make it stop
Please make it stop

I used to be sane, rational
Now I'm losing my mind
I jump at my own shadow
I run from everything

I don't know where I am
What I'm doing
Who I am
What I am

Help me, help me please
My head pounds, my heart races
I want to end this, I have to end this


CAN'T...TAKE...THIS...ANYMORE!

**BLAM!**

# VOICES PT. 2

I hear voices in my head
Ancestors speaking
Children crying
Women screaming

My mind explodes with the sounds
I wonder why me
Why was I summoned?
Why do they speak to me?

Sojourner Truth says run
Run and be free
Rosa parks riding for freedom
I will not be moved

Children losing their lives
The 4 little girls of Alabama
Trayvon Martin, Jordan Davis
Emmitt till lynched

Shots fired our heroes slain
Martin, Malcolm gone
Medgar Evers slain at home
Fred Hampton murdered in his bed

These voices I hear in my head
 I wonder why me
Why was I summoned?
Why do they speak to me?

*Anthony Arnold*

# WATERFALLS

I stand under the cleansing waterfall
Letting the pain of the past fall away
My soul becoming whole
Once again

I feel life return to me
My spirit uplifted
The voices of the ancestors
Fill me with joy

The water runs red with the blood of those gone before
Lynched and slain
Men women and children
Some never seen again

I see their tears washed away
In the eternal flow
Their pain and agony
Cleansed

As I stand here, my tears blend with the flow
My heart beating, my soul shining
Reaching out to the future
Holding on to the past

# WATTS

*(It's a black community, no one cares)*

An arrest, a suspected DUI
Mother called, arguments ensue
Fights break out, unrest starts
And then it begins

It's a black community, no one cared

Housing discrimination, no jobs
Only available, south side Los Angeles
Nowhere else are they allowed
Nowhere else can they stay

It's a black community, no one cared

Police brutality, the thin blue line
We are in control
Men and women, blacks and Latinos
We are the LAPD

It's a black community, no one cared

August 11, 1965. All hell breaks loose
National Guard called, chaos
Acting like monkeys in a zoo, the chief says
It's a black community, no one cared

1000 buildings, 40 mil gone
It's in a black community, no one cared
No housing, no jobs, no fair schools
It's in a black community, no one cares

It was just another arrest, said the cop
Just another day at the office
A son and a mother arrested
It's in a black community, no one cares

*Anthony Arnold*

Its 2014, and the struggle remains
Look around few things have changed
The towers look over those who remain
The more things change, the more they stay the same

# WILLIE LYNCH

*(Or the separation of black America)*

We all know who Willie lynch is
Author of that damned letter
But he didn't realize was
Willie was preaching to the choir

From the beginning we were our own worst enemy
Our own slavers
Selling our people into bondage
For trinkets. For a piece of gold

We were and are our own worst enemy
Turn them against each other
Your work will be done
You job will be done for you

Set them upon themselves
Field niggas vs. house niggas
Light skinned vs. dark skinned
Young vs. old

You don't need to beat or maim
To kill serve no purpose
Give them a reason to hate
Make them resent each other

Today it still resonates
Don't believe me look around
Light skinned vs. dark skinned
Processed (weave) vs. natural

It's screamed from the media
Wannabees; wannabe better than me
Nappy heads; pro natural
School daze anyone?

99

_Anthony Arnold_

1712 to 2013, and we still haven't learned
We just don't get it
Those who don't know their history are doomed to repeat it
We are living proof

People it is time to get up
Help each other up
Raise your voices
And scream...

WAKE  UP!!!!!!!!!

# MY MUSE

She came to me in a dream
An angel dressed in white
What is the matter my son
Your voice has gone silent

I cannot write
My muse is gone
I have no words
My ink is cold

She was my rock
My Gibraltar
A life line
A port in any storm

She was my biggest fan
My ardent supporter
She would tell anyone
These words came from my son

Your words are needed
Your faith in your people
A beacon of hope
A life an example

Who am I to speak out?
To criticize injustice
To educate anyone
To bring ancestors to life

If one is touched
If one is enlightened
If one is helped
Your task is done

Looking at the angel

With tears falling
Who am I to speak?
How do I express my heart?

With a smile that brightened the heavens
And a voice that rang with music
She took my hand and said

My son you already have

RIP my muse
Marolyn Martin
1942-2014

# ON THE STREETS

*(Life Imitates Art)*

A voice behind me said
Please don't call the cops
I'll move if you want me too
This is my home

Looking at this small white haired woman
I smiled at her and said
Your fine, you're on the street
You're not on my property

She smiled and replied thank you
If you call they will impound it
And take it away from me
My tags are expired

I watched as she prepared her van for the night
When she finished she said, good night young man
I feel safer knowing that you are out here
Good night

I gazed as she locked herself in
I wondered how I would feel
Knowing that I had a mother
Living in a vehicle

This is someone's mother
Grandmother
Living, no existing nowhere to go
In a van.

On the street.

#iammybrotherkeeper
#watchingoverhertonight

*Anthony Arnold*

# SOCIAL CONFUSION

Our society seems to be in a state of confusion
Do you know where we're going? Where we're headed
The rich get richer, the poorer get poorer
And the rest are caught in the middle

Socialism, capitalism, democracy, and communism
None is better than the other, none is worse
We are all robbing peter to pay Paul
And it all goes in a vicious circle

Wasn't things supposed to be getting better
They couldn't get any worse
Pretty soon we'll all be standing on the corner with a sign
Can I get some change to pay my bills?

Wars have been fought, lives have been lost
All for the weapons of mass confusion
That we sent our men and women to find
And they have come home more confused or dead

Like the Temptations said," The world is a ball of confusion"
Nothing changes it goes round and round
One day maybe we will find out where the world is headed
But until then the band plays on

# A STORM IS COMING PT. 2

An ill wind is blowing
The storm is here
It bodes not well
The future is bleak

Florida, Michigan, Cali
Chicago Ferguson, New York
We are falling like flies
Yet no one can tell us why

Driving while black, walking while black
Living while black, no difference is made
The common denominator is
We exist. We are black

Like Marvin said, there are too many mothers crying
This isn't Vietnam
But our cities are becoming war zones
Again, here comes the National Guard

To serve and protect
To kill and reject
I am unarmed
Please don't shoot

Homicide, genocide, my ride or die died
We hate on our own
We are like a predator,
We eat our own

We have to learn to survive
Our future depends on it
Our past needs it
Our ancestors demand it

*Anthony Arnold*

The winds of change are a hurricane
The storm is here.
What do we do now?
How will we survive?

# RUNNING

He hears the sounds of gunfire in the distance
His heart pounds, his breath labored
Yet to survive he has to keep going
He has to keep running

His homeland torn with violence
Children dead or dying
Civil war all he's ever known
Family. Friends gone

Escape from the camp he's called home
To the border, to safety he goes
Another life, another time
Running to freedom

Night and day, day and night he runs
For his life he runs
For his freedom he runs
For his future he runs

A lost boy of Sudan, he's called
A child with no home
To live he must get away
To survive he is forever

Running

*Anthony Arnold*

# SEEDS OF DESTRUCTION

Hatred greed jealousy
Our past eradicated
The tree of woe blossoms
The seeds of destruction sown

Rosewood, Fl. All black, self sufficient
Thriving on its own
But by misinformation, mob mentality
All is left to tell the tale is a sign

Black Wall Street, Middle class divine
Everything we needed, we owned
Jealousy and greed reared its head
Nothing left but a visitor's center

We destroy our own
Yet what does it serve
Is there any change?
Any justice, any peace?

Detroit, Liberty city, LA, Ferguson
Home, businesses, lives lost
Yet there was no relief
Lady Justice was and is blind

The seeds bear fruit
We contribute to our own demise
Yet while the destruction flows around us
We have the power to chop down the tree

Hatred greed jealousy
Our past eradicated
The tree of woe blossoms
The seeds of destruction sown

# STREET LIFE

(Inspired by the music of Joe Sample)

Street Life

Another day in the life
Survival of the fittest
We do what we can
Just to live another day

Children playing, screaming
Tapping fire hydrants
Mothers crying
Another child gone

Street life

Homeless on the street
Looking for a nickel, for a dime
People walk by, noses in the air
Not knowing that once he was just like them

Ladies of the night, doin the do
Streetwalkers trying to make it right
No one knows at night when she goes home
She has mouths to feed

Street Life

Pimps and pushers, crack heads all around
Yo man I'll suck you off for a rock
Respectable people they used to be
Getting hooked is a bitch

Got to get yours before they get theirs
By any means necessary
Sometimes you don't make it
Sometimes neither do they

*Anthony Arnold*

Street life

Another day in the life
Survival of the fittest
We do what we can
Just to live another day

RIP Joe sample
2/1/1939-9/12/2014

# EXPRESSIONS

History has a voice that has become silent over the years. With each passing day, the generations lose sight of what people fought and died to give them today. Your writing touches a deep part of the soul. It stirs that part within that says, 'We cannot forget where we came from and what was lost to make today possible.' You keep our eyes focused and our hearts linked to passages of time that we shall share for generations to come! ~ Sheila Moseley

One of the many challenges of any poet, is to have their work read. We have the luxury of being online and having access to many a fine poet, Anthony Arnold stands out amongst the many, his direction is clear, and his poetry distinguishes itself from many others. From social issues, to a lone lily in the field, Mr. Anthony Arnold's pen will capture and put to word what his readers feel. ~ Joe DaVerbalMindancer

The first time I read the works of Mr. Anthony Arnold, I was instantly taken aback by his sheer genius in his way of painting visual images through his lyrical expression! This gentleman is the epitome of the original storytellers! Each time I am privileged to read his work, it's like I was a fly on the wall witnessing an awesome adventure. ~ Allen Simmons

Anthony Arnold, has been expressing his unlimited talents in writing and scholastic achievements for as long as I've known him. He's captured my mind, soul and spirit to become open, never to forget our life experiences, we've learned by living through our history growing up whether in the foreign countries, generations from slavery, to the Hood tales! He brings it out of us.

Anthony Arnold can reach you by guiding you into Love, Family Unity, Government laws, and even the Military where he served victoriously...and I Salute him and everyone whom served!

He is the most diligent and prepared person I've ever known.

I've purchased his first two books: 1). MY PEOPLE, OUR TRIALS AND TRIBULATIONS. 2). URBAN MUSINGS: COME TAKE A WALK IN MY HOOD. I am anticipating the new read of his latest book!

Thank you Author Anthony Arnold, for opening my heart to never letting me forget my Urban People past and present! ~ Jacqueline D. Kennedy aka Shihi Venus

# ANTHONY ARNOLD

Anthony Arnold, born and raised by his grandmother in a little town called Quincy in Florida, wrote his first piece in the third grade and fell in love with writing ever since that moment; writing has become a comfort and a mainstay to keep him focused. As an avid reader of all genres of literature, Anthony has found a particular passion for black history.

He believes that his ancestry and the ones that have come before him have given their blood sweat and tears to make it possible for him to live a life of freedom and liberation. Anthony is saddened to the fact that the current generation lacks knowledge and don't seem to know or speak of family history, our history or black history.

Writing gives Anthony the ability to educate those that have no clue about the things that African Americans have faced and write of things that they will never be taught in schools, such as "African

Americans" and the Civil War and shedding light on the strength of our people.

Anthony's love for fellow man grew during his service to our country where he served and was awarded numerous medals, including Air Force Achievement Medal-1986, 1993 and 2001 and many more.

His desire to show the younger generation to want to learn about where they come from and to let them know we are much more than what society has labeled us!

Anthony Arnold
USA
African American
Born: May 4, 1961, Tampa, FL

www.ingramcontent.com/pod-product-compliance
Lightning Source LLC
Chambersburg PA
CBHW032042040426
42449CB00007B/985